HISTORIC HOMES

OF THE

ISLE OF MAN

Compiled by

John Kitto

*This book is dedicated to the
memory of the late Mona Douglas without whose
diligent researches it would never have been conceived
let alone published*

Published by Executive Publications and
printed by Print Centres Limited
Spring Valley Industrial Estate, Braddan, Isle of Man
1990

ISBN 0 9516846 0 4 Hardback
0 9516846 1 2 Paperback

FOREWORD

There are no stately homes as such in the Isle of Man and currently only one private house is open to the public on a regular basis. But there are many homes which have an interesting history.

We have called the book 'Historic Homes . . . ' rather than 'Historic Houses . . . ' as of course nearly all of the buildings shown have been extensively modernised or rebuilt wholly or in part since they were first erected.

Those shown in this book by no means represent the full complement and, of those which appear, several are illustrated only by old prints or old photographs from the Manx Museum or elsewhere. In one case, Rectory House, Andreas, this is because the house is currently undergoing extensive renovation. In all other cases, however, it is because their owners have declined to grant our request to photograph the exterior of their houses.

Our warmest thanks and appreciation go to the majority of householders who did allow their homes to be photographed — in some cases internally as well as externally — and for the great help they gave in showing their records, house deeds, old photographs, etc. Our thanks also go to the Manx Museum library for all the help, prints and old photographs which they unearthed and allowed us to reproduce.

PREFACE

Soon after I started the first of the Island's glossy magazines in 1971, the then proprietor of its printing and publishing house had the idea of producing a book on some of the more interesting houses of the Isle of Man. As the late Mona Douglas was at that time looking for more freelance work, she was commissioned to research the history of a number of them through the Manx Museum, General Registry, etc.

Before he could do anything about publishing the proposed book, the proprietor was obliged to return to live in England and so, just prior to his departure, he handed me all the research notes, telling me to do what I liked with them!

Until I retired in 1985, they remained at the back of a drawer. But thereafter, when the mood took me, I wrote up the notes into normal prose and typed them up. During the course of 1990, I completed the task and, having found a publisher, took all the exterior colour photographs during the unbroken sunshine in July.

I hope you will find the result as interesting as I did when writing up the notes, even though you cannot enjoy the additional advantage I had of meeting the many delightful people living in the houses I photographed.

John Kitto,
Fernside,
Glen Auldyn,
Lezayre,
Isle of Man.

CONTENTS

(cont.)

CONTENTS *(cont.)*

Arragon House, Santon

Arragon House, until comparatively recently an hotel, has accomplished the curious feat of being generally known by three different names at successive periods and finally reverting, more or less by accident, to the oldest one recorded. It is part of a large and very old holding of which the original name was Ard Roagan, or Roagan's Height. Sometime in the sixteenth century this estate was divided, and half of it took the name of Ballavilley; then in the eighteenth century, on the marriage of its heiress, Ann Cosnahan, to the father of Major Caesar Bacon, CP, JP, MHK, Ballavilley itself was again divided, and Major Bacon gave to his portion the name of Seafield, by which it was known until fairly recently. The other half of the property retained the name of Ballavilley and the original estate that of Arragon, as it still does. It is believed to have been Major Caesar Bacon who built the present house.

The Bacons claimed descent from a Roman doctor who came to the Island in the reign of Queen Elizabeth I, and have retained the name Caesar for at least one son of the family in each generation. There is also a tradition that they were closely associated in Rome with the ruling house, and the drawing room at Seafield used to be lined with portraits of the Roman emperors. Members of the family lived there until the first quarter of the present century, but finally it was sold to be converted into an hotel, and after this purchase the hotel took 'Arragon' as its trade name, but altered the pronunciation, which placed the accent correctly on the second syllable, to the Anglicised 'Arragon'. It is now once again a private house.

Photo: Manx Museum & National Trust

A view of Seafield House, later called Arragon House

Ballachurry, Andreas

Ballachurry has been for many generations the seat of the Crellins, one of the old northside families who have played a prominent part in Manx affairs for centuries and still do.

The estate is chiefly remarkable for its number of antiquarian remains, notably a prehistoric earth fort and another fine, well preserved one of the seventeenth century which was erected in 1640 by the seventh Earl of Derby. It was never occupied for military purposes, though such occupation was contemplated as part of the northern defences during the Manx rebellion of 1651.

Ballacotch Manor, Marown

T he exact origins of Ballacotch Manor are a bit of a mystery. It seems likely that some of it which still forms a part of the existing building dates back to the fifteenth century. Other parts are at least two hundred years old. At one time it was known and marked on maps as Hope Lodge and was probably used by one of the Manx Lieutenant Governors of that name as a weekend retreat. Yet there is a reference in the title deeds to the manor being a part of the estates of Ballacotch *and* Hope Lodge.

The deeds however only go back one hundred years when, in the first recorded sale of Hope Lodge, 'formerly called Ballacotch', it went for the sum of £2,600. At that time the estate comprised about 36 acres, but five fields were added to it in 1925, bringing it up to its present extent of 50 acres.

In more recent times it has been in the ownership of the Cunningham family, being purchased by Harley Cunningham (of holiday camp fame) in 1944, and sold by his second wife in 1959 to W. L. & J. Cowin. They in turn sold it in 1961 with its grounds and two cottages to Leslie Cussons (known best for his firm which produces soap and other toilet preparations), and he lived there until his death in 1963.

The extensive modernisation and the vast improvement of the garden and parkland have made it one of the Island's outstanding estates. The house itself is built on gently sloping ground which shelters it from the south west wind but gives it a north facing frontage which overlooks Glen Vine towards the high ground above the Baldwin valley.

Photo: Manx Museum & National Trust

Balladoole House, Rushen

Balladoole House is one of the oldest continuously occupied estates in the Island. The name originated in the fourteenth century, when it was owned by a Galloway chieftain named Lord Duncan MacDowell. At that time a common Gaelic was spoken in the Island and all up the west coast of Scotland, including Galloway where it survived in common speech until well into the last century; and the Gaelic form of MacDowell would be Mac Dubhghall, pronounced more or less like 'Doo-all', and this later became 'Doole', the Mac prefix being dropped. In 1307, Lord Duncan MacDowell owned not only the whole Treen of Balladoole but also the Calf of Man, and was connected with the Manx royal line. In 1334, Gilbert mac Stephan, custodian of Castle Rushen, married the MacDowell heiress and inherited Balladoole, and the Stevenson family held the estate until 1972, though the original dwelling house is now only a grassy mound in the garden, about a hundred yards from the existing house. In 1837, a silver seal was found on that site bearing the Stevenson coat of arms which experts pronounced to be 'at least 400 years old'.

The present Balladoole House was built in 1714 by Mr. John Stevenson, the first recorded Speaker of the House of Keys, and it has hardly been altered structurally since then. It is a fine example of the Queen Anne period in architecture, and has been carefully and extensively restored by successive owners. The most important part of the early restoration was renovation of the very beautiful woodwork, and a special showpiece is the lovely Queen Anne staircase.

Photo: Manx Museum & National Trust

Balladoole House showing its original pillared front

13

The original Ballamannaugh Beg farmhouse

Ballamannaugh, Sulby

It is not at all unusual to find two adjacent farms in a Manx parish bearing the same name, and a distinction is made by calling one Moar (big) and the other Beg (little), or sometimes East and West. Both these things have happened to the original Ballamannaugh, Lezayre, though not officially on the maps.

In the early 1930s Sir Mark Collet, a distinguished Manxman who had worked for many years in the public life of England, decided to come back to his ancestral Island to retire, and bought Ballamannaugh, Sulby, just under the ancient fort of Cronk Sumark. His first intention was to pull down and rebuild, or to modernise, the old farmhouse, but he eventually decided to leave this attractive old house alone and build a new and larger one further up the Cronk, with extensive

An attractive woodland feature near to the old Ballamannaugh Beg farmhouse

The modern Ballamannaugh

gardens, gardening being a favourite hobby of both himself and his wife, Lady Violet.

The result is one of the most delightful and well sited modern houses in the Island, with gardens which are a showpiece of the north. Sensibly, however, he decided to retain the old farmhouse, which is both characteristic and charming. He also retained the name Ballamannaugh for his new house, and this has led to the unofficial renaming of the farm house, for local people now speak of Ballamannaugh and Ballamannaugh Beg. The name itself is a very old one, meaning Estate of the Monks, for the original Ballamannaugh was used by the Rushen Abbey monks (the whole Treen is Abbey Land) as their northern headquarters and house of hospitality on their itinerary of the Abbey Lands; and from Cronk Sumark the old monastic track leads over the mountains southward to Rushen Abbey.

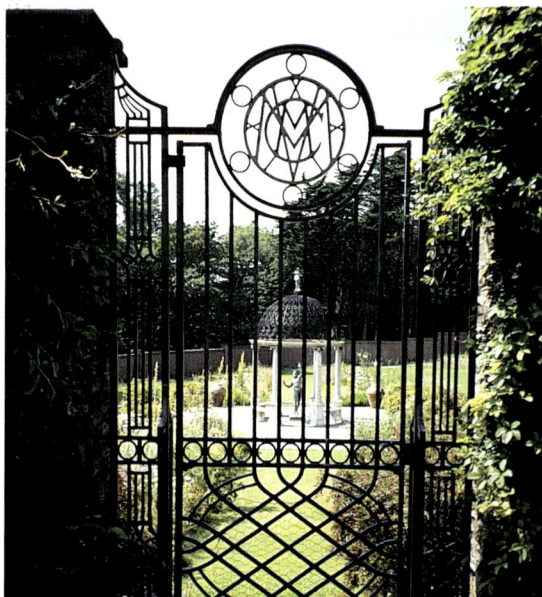

The gardens are a showpiece of the north

Ballamoar Castle, Jurby

Ballamoar Castle is one of those houses which are modern but do not look it. In fact, the present mansion house was built in 1905; but it stands on the site of an older and much more modest one which was for centuries the home of a northside family whose members have been an integral part of Manx history, and which was known simply as Ballamoar. The Christians of Ballamoar were a branch of that important family which produced Deemsters and other top-ranking officials from medieval times onward; and the last of them to live in Ballamoar was William Christian, Receiver General of the Island, who married Ann, daughter of Deemster Mylrea in 1706 and died in 1757. Their daughter married Richard Moore of Pulrose, and his daughter Margaret, who inherited Ballamoar, married Robert Farrant, who became the first Farrant of Ballamoar and died there in 1820. In 1822 their son, William Farrant, married Susannah E. Curphey, the heiress of Ballakillingan, Lezayre, and he is the man who has left his mark most indelibly on the estate, for he travelled widely.

The beautifully carved wood pannelling in the dining room

From 1896 onward he made it his chief hobby to bring to Ballamoar and plant there specimens of rare and beautiful trees, shrubs and other plants which he collected from far-off lands. The Ballamoar park and gardens are famous for their remarkable number and variety of species of trees, including the rare Himalayan Falconer's rhododendron, of which the Ballamoar specimen is said to be the largest in Europe.

The house itself is beautifully sited on a terrace at the top of a long gentle slope. There is a magnificent sweep of lawns which form an ideal setting for the rare and lovely trees, and beyond these stretch wilder woodlands and small streams carpeted in the spring with bluebells and other wild flowers. The grounds cover an area of about 50 acres altogether. There are also walled flower and vegetable gardens, but these have, wisely, been kept to a separate site behind the house.

Ranged around the yard at the back are stables and coach-house (now a garage), a laundry and a workshop, and beyond the yard is the entrance to the walled garden.

In 1900 Ballamoar was owned by Alfred George Curphey, and it was he who had the old farmhouse demolished and the present mansion built in the Gothic style by Messrs. Kelly Brothers. In 1908 he sold it to Baron Francois Rom, a wealthy Belgian manufacturer, but during the 1914-1918 war, Baron Rom had most of his property destroyed by the Germans and was forced to sell Ballamoar.

It was bought by John Duncan Blackwell, and since then has had several owners including the remarkable Dr. Cannon, who introduced himself as Dr. Sir Alexander Cannon, Kushog Yogi of Tibet, KGCB, MD, DPM, MA(Cantab), PhD, FRGS. Accused (unjustly) of being a spy, it was felt he was living too close to the RAF airfield at Jurby and was obliged to sell Ballamoar — he renamed it Ballamoar Castle — soon after buying it in 1939.

It was purchased by the Shimwell family in 1953 and has remained in their possession ever since.

The main reception rooms face south overlooking the wide sweep of lawn

Ballamoar Farm, Patrick

Ballamoar Farm was the seat of Sir George Moore, born 1709, who was the Speaker of the House of Keys and the national leader of the Manx resistance to a proposal made at the time of the Revestment to annex the Island to Cumberland. He secured from the British Government a recognition of Manx independence in the terms of the revised Constitution.

His grandson, Philip Moore, who also held Ballamoar, was a close friend of the Duke of Atholl who was then Lord of Mann, and interested His Grace in several projects for the benefit of the Island, notably the improvement of the harbour works at Douglas. The Duke used to stay overnight at Ballamoar before the annual Tynwald Ceremony, go to it from there, and return to dine there afterwards.

In 1838 the estate was sold for £7,800 and since then it has had several owners, including an Icelander named Oddson who farmed it after World War II until 1951.

Ballaquane, Peel

This was originally a farmhouse, and the oldest part of the building, still incorporated in the structure, has been there for well over 200 years. In the 1820s it was owned by the Cowell family, one of whom, Mr John Cowell, was Captain of the Parish of German. He died at Ballaquane in 1828, and his son inherited the estate. Over the door was a plaque with the date 1798, but whether this recorded the first building of the house or a later extension is uncertain.

In 1890 it was bought and virtually rebuilt in Elizabethan style by the late High Bailiff Laughton, who lived there until well into the second decade of the present century. In the 1920s it was occupied by Mr Frank Lightowler, a well known sculptor, and in 1935 it was bought and occupied by the late Speaker of the House of Keys, Mr H K Corlett, but was divided into two separate portions.

There is a strong tradition in Peel that Ballaquane, or part of it, was at one time a public house, but no definite information seems to be available as to when this was, or what its name was. Peel people, however, still know what is now officially Ballaquane Road as Brewery Road.

Ballaughton, Braddan

Ballaughton, originally a quarterland, is one of the old Baronial Estates of the Island, which in 1580 was held by one Henry Crye and known as Ballacrye. In 1583 John Aghton became the owner and gave his name to the estate. Thenceforward it was known as Balla Aghton, which inevitably came to be pronounced Ball'Aghton, and later Ballaughton as at present. A curious feature of the name is that owing to the introduction at some time of the 'u' before the personal name, it seems to have been associated with the parish name Ballaugh, and the 'gh' at the end is now pronounced like 'f' instead of its original slightly guttural pronunciation.

In 1585 the quarterland was divided into two equal parts, one owned by the Corkill family and known as Ballaughton Corkill; the other owned by the Curleods and known as Ballaughton Curleod. The Corkills held their half until 1808, when it was sold to Mungo Murray for £4,157. Murray belonged to an old Douglas family of merchants who, in the year 1690, issued the first Manx coin,

The entrance hall

23

The sitting room faces east and south overlooking the spacious garden

called Murray's Pence. In 1813 Mungo Murray sold part of his Ballaughton holding to the Duke of Atholl for £500, and in 1820 he sold another portion of it to Sir Mark Wilks for the same price. In 1824 the Duke sold his portion to John Wulff of Liverpool for £5,000, and in 1846 G. W. Dumbell, who was Wulff's executor, sold the same portion to Samuel Harris for £7,420. It was later re-transferred to Dumbell.

The other half-quarterland, Ballaughton Curleod, remained in the Curleod family until 1805. In 1825 Harrison of the Woodbourne Estate purchased it for £5,000, and within the following 25 years both Harcroft and Springfield, two attractive family villa residences were built on the land. In 1859 William Beckwith of Glencrutchery purchased Harcroft for £1,850 and in 1881 Springfield was sold to Mr. L. Vulliamy for £2,000.

After the last war Ballaughton became the residence of one of the most prominent Manxmen of our time, the late Deemster Sir Percy Cowley. Thereafter, in 1959, it was the home of Major T. E. Brownsdon OBE, a Manxman with many Island interests.

The dining room

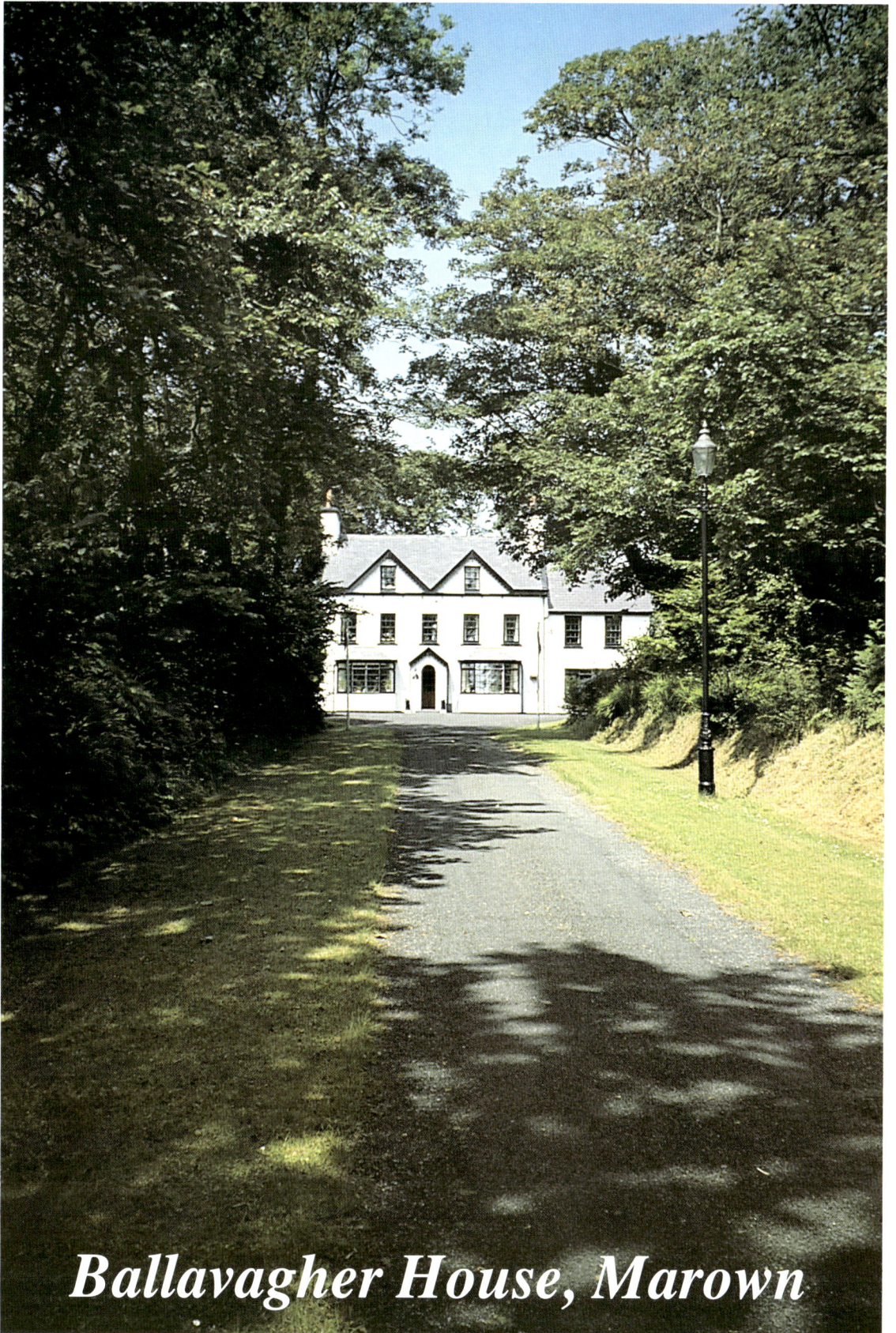

Ballavagher House, Marown

Ballavagher House, Marown

Ballavagher House

At various periods the house has been let. In 1806 a newspaper reported that Captain Grice of the Loyal Manx Volunteers had died at Ballavagher and a sale was being held of his household furniture and effects. Between 1813 and 1825, newspaper advertisements indicated that Mr. and Mrs. T. Howard were tenants, and in 1815 they were offering country lodgings at Ballavagher. During 1825 the house and garden were twice advertised for letting.

It is said that one of the owners in Victorian times, a parson, incurred much displeasure through taking and using old gravestones to provide gateposts on the farm.

Ballavagher, comprising the mansion house and its surrounding farm, is an ancient holding whose land boundaries have possibly remained unchanged since Viking days.

The oldest buildings on the estate are the farmhouse and farm buildings, which were originally thatched and are of an earlier style than is generally found on the Island.

The mansion house, which is approached through a fine avenue of trees, was built about two hundred years ago, probably by the Gelling family who remained in possession of the estate until 1965.

The attractive garden at the rear of Ballavagher House

In latter years, successors of the Gelling family were again unable to live at Ballavagher for various reasons, and the house became a Youth Hostel. It then lay empty for some while in an increasingly dilapidated condition until the estate was sold in 1964. The house has since been extensively altered and renovated in keeping with its character.

A sundial on the front porch, inscribed P K 1853, was made by a member of the Kewley family of neighbouring Ballafreer, who were well-known makers of sundials.

The Farmhouse

Ballavale, Santon

Ballavale was known as Balnahowin until 1703, and in this form it appears in the Manorial Roll for 1511, when it was held by one Fynlo McQua; but at that time the dwelling house was of the usual small Manx farmhouse type, and there does not appear to be any record of the exact date when it was altered and enlarged. In 1820 the estate was advertised in the *Manx Advertiser* for letting and described as 'About 100 acres, with mansion house and offices'. It apparently belonged then to the Rev. John Nelson, as in September of that year there is a report in the same newspaper of Henry Quayle 'steward to the Rev. John Nelson' being killed in an accident at Ballavale. In 1831 the *Manx Sun* carried a notice of the marriage of a daughter of 'Philip Kinley of Ballavale, Santon' and in 1835 the estate was again advertised for letting.

Billown, Malew

Billown is a very old estate and was formerly Bylozen, in which form it appears in the Chronicle of Man written by the monks of Rushen Abbey in the twelfth and thirteenth centuries. The name has been classified as Gaelicized Norse, and must always have been a holding of some importance as the prefix 'By' was only given to superior estates. Its original meaning would be 'Lhodinn's Farm', and in later times the name Lhodinn would in the Manx Gaelic speech become something like Lowdhin which still later would merge into Lown.

Though Billown was apparently a place of importance in Norse times, according to some archaeologists it was in still earlier times a temple and settlement of a prehistoric religion, traces of which remain in Billown stone circle. This was formerly supposed to be a burial place; later excavation, however, showed that there were no indications of burials but many signs of human occupation and the use of fire. Some believe it to have been connected with sun worship and the Belthane fire ceremonies.

The estate, one of the largest in the Island, was for several centuries the property of the Moore family, though this is no longer so. The original house was probably built in the seventeenth century, but was burnt down and replaced by the present building which at the time of going to press was undergoing extensive renovation and modernisation.

Bishopscourt, Michael

Bishopscourt is probably the only existing building in the Island which has been in continuous occupation from the early thirteenth century by record and at least a century earlier by tradition. Until recent times it was the official residence of the Lord Bishops of Sodor and Man. Some additions and alterations have been made during the intervening centuries, naturally, but the central portion, known as the Orry Tower is unaltered structurally.

From 1154 the Bishopric was under the Scandinavian hierarchy of the Church with its metropolitan see in Trondheim, and to the Manx people of that time, mostly Celts who had partially assimilated Norse settlers, it would seem natural to couple the spiritual head of the nation with the King and to assign the rights to both in the chief dwelling place of the land, as they sat together in equality on the summit of Tynwald Hill for the annual law-giving ceremony. The

The Straton Hall, named after Bishop Straton

tradition is that the tower was first built as a military work of defence and residence for the King, and that later, when Christianity became the State religion, the Bishop was allocated the landward facing half while the King retained the part facing towards the sea.

The earliest record we have, however, is of a Bishop in residence, with no reference to the King. He was Bishop Simon, famous for many religious reforms and enterprises; especially for having initiated the plan to build St. German's Cathedral on Inis Patrick and almost completing the building during his term as Bishop, which was from 1226 to 1247. He is recorded in the *Chronicon Manniae* as having died on the last day of February 1247, 'at the Church of St. Michael the Archangel' — the parish church of Bishopscourt. One would like to know how it came about that the Bishop died there instead of at his residence, but the Chronicle gives no details. There was an ancient chapel at Bishopscourt on the site of the present one, but this is said also to have been dedicated to St. Nicholas. The Manx parishes were only formed late in the twelfth century however, and with the Bishop actually resident in the Parish of Michael it is unlikely that there would be also a resident vicar, so perhaps Bishop Simon died while or after serving Mass.

The old tower used to be surrounded by a moat, part of which can still be traced, and some prints of it made in about 1640 show that in addition to it there were two wings, and a bell swung from the battlements.

The north east section of the Peele Tower forms a spacious drawing room

The panelling and fireplace in the dining room are both original, the latter displaying Straton's episcopal coat of arms

A list of the interior rooms and domestic offices made in 1788 when extensive repairs were undertaken reads: 'The Hall, the Parlour, the Little Parlour, the Pantry, the Kitchen, the Small Beer Cellar, the Wine Binns, the Wainscoted Bedroom and the room over it, the Stone Staircase to the Tower, the Wig Room, the Bishops Bedroom, the Study, the Herring Cellar, the Wooden Shed for turf, the Brew House and Coal House, the Grainery and Pidgeon House, the Goose Yard and the Pig House.'

The Chapel was restored in 1854 and some further additions have been made since then to the dwelling, but externally the old Peele or Orry tower and the surrounding grounds with their many fine trees still retain the character of past centuries.

An illustrated booklet on the complete history of Bishopscourt may be obtained on the premises which are open to the public during the summer.

A charming feature in the gardens

Bolivia Mount, Andreas

Bolivia Mount was built in 1851 by Philip Teare, who had lived for a considerable time in Bolivia, and like a good many Manxmen who had made money abroad, retired in later life to his native Island and called the house he built for himself after the country where he had found his fortune. The house commands one of the finest views in the north of the Island, being built on a small hill rising out of flat country, but it was not originally Bolivia Mount — just Bolivia. Then several smaller houses around were called names like Bolivia Cottage, and the 'Mount' was added to distinguish the mansion house. The Teares lived there until 1875. In 1884, Hugh Sanderson Playfair of Melbourne, Australia, was the owner and put the house up for sale. There is a gap in the available records until 1919 when John Henry Quayle of Southport bought it, and apparently owned it until 1941.

Bridge House, Castletown

Bridge House is one of the most famous dwelling places in the Island. For centuries it was the citadel of the Quayles, a family involved in most of the important events of Manx history and also known for the enterprise, originality and independence of various members. They were probably there on the site when the Kingdom of Mann and the Isles flourished, but the first record we have is that a Quayle of Castletown was a Member of the House of Keys in 1422, and four of the family have been Clerks of the Rolls. Their earliest residence has disappeared but the oldest part of the present house was built in the early years of the eighteenth century and was much lower than it is today — and thereby hangs a tale. In 1809 George Quayle, the then head of the family, was contemplating extensions of the house when it came to his ears that His Excellency the Lieutenant Governor was also having some extensions made to Lorne House (then Government House) which would enable him to overlook Bridge House. The Quayles have always been exclusive, especially in respect of the English ascendancy, and George protested against what he considered an invasion of his privacy. A full scale row ensued, and the solution of the matter he adopted was to extend Bridge House upward instead of on ground level as he had originally intended. As a result the extension not only blocked the view from Lorne House of Castletown Bay but also prevented a lot of sunlight from reaching its greenhouses.

Bridge House has been a bank, a headquarters of the Manx Yeomanry Cavalry, and by tradition also a centre for the free trade which the English regarded as smuggling but the Manx maintained was perfectly legal according to Manx law. One of the most famous Manx ships, the schooner *Peggy* was built for George Quayle and a boathouse-cum-clubroom was built especially for her at Bridge House. The clubroom was used for private parties and also for meetings of the Royal and Ancient Order of Bucks, of which George Quayle was a prominent member. This was a body which was partly social but also had political interests of a decidedly nationalist character. George was a strong Manx patriot and, when offered a knighthood by the English government, he declined it. On several occasions he opposed the Duke of Atholl, then Lord of Mann, on matters affecting the welfare of the Manx people, and carried his point.

Quayle's Bank was opened in Bridge House in March 1802, and its notes were considered as good as those of the Bank of England. A special strong room was constructed in Bridge House which had a burglar trap invented by George Quayle himself, who had among other talents a flair for mechanical inventions. The *Peggy* and her boathouse have been acquired by the Manx Museum, having been presented to the Museum Trustees by the Quayle family descendants when Bridge House was sold in February 1942. After the last war they were restored, and opened as a Nautical Museum in 1951. This small museum was considerably enlarged in 1967. Bridge House was unoccupied for some time after the death of the last of the Quayles to live there, but today it is again inhabited.

The 'Peggy' in her boat house

Crogga as it is today

Crogga & Ballashamrock House, Braddan

The adjacent estates of Crogga and Ballashamrock House were both owned for something like a hundred years by the well known Quayle family of Castletown. In the eighteenth century when the Manx contraband trade was at its peak and smuggling was no offence under Manx law, both houses were used openly as convenient places to store 'trade' goods, for Port Soderick was a favourite landing place. In 1736 the British Customs Protection Act resulted in the increase of revenue cutters patrolling the Manx coast and made landings more difficult, and in 1765 the British Government compelled the Duke of Atholl to surrender his Lordship of Mann to the Crown for £70,000 — a compulsory purchase deal which both he and the Manx people resented — and the contraband trade was made illegal in this Island as well as in England. It still continued, for most of the leading Manx families were deeply involved in it and getting considerable profit from it — including the Quayles. These two estates were then still more

The original building in the Crogga grounds

39

important, for landings were made by night and it was only a very short distance to convey the goods to them in darkness. They were hidden there until they could be moved on, again by night. The Quayles never occupied either of these houses, but they had stewards living there — who were also their agents in 'The Trade.' In 1822 the steward living in Crogga was one William Hunter, a Scot, and it was probably he who added or got his employer to add the Scottish Baronial type of frontage to Crogga House, which was formerly a plain Manx farmhouse very much like the Ballashamrock House. Crogga and Ballashamrock are both very appropriately sited above Port Soderick Glen which leads directly to the shore.

Ballashamrock House

40

Cronkbourne, Braddan

C ronkbourne was formerly part of the Quarterland of Ballafletcher in the Treen of Castle Ward, and was created a separate estate in the early nineteenth century under its present name. At this period and in the preceding century there was a vogue among property owners, mainly those who were new residents, to change the existing names of old Manx properties to completely new English ones; but in this case the owner, a Manxman named Moore, seems to have compromised by combining a Manx and an English word, Cronk being Manx Gaelic for Hill and Bourne an English word for a river or small stream. There is no record of an earlier name for this house, and it appears as Cronk Bourne in newspaper advertisements of 1831.

The house's interior was designed by Ewan Christian, an architect who was a descendant of William Christian (Illiam Dhône) and in the same line of descent from Fletcher Christian of

The dining room

The entrance hall. The impressive fireplace commemorates the visits of Edward VII in 1902 and of Prince George in 1932.

'*Bounty*' fame. Ewan subsequently became architect to the Church Commissioners and was President of the Royal Institute of British Architects from 1884 to 1886.

Cronkbourne was the seat of the Moore family until comparatively recently and for many years was the home of one of the most notable of modern Manxmen, Arthur William Moore, Speaker of the House of Keys, scholar, historian and folk-lorist. After his death it became the home of his successor as Speaker, Mr. G. F. Clucas, who was also a well known Manx scholar. It has been honoured by more than one royal visit.

The fireplace in the billiards room was designed by Sir Edward Burn-Jones

Druidale Farm, Michael

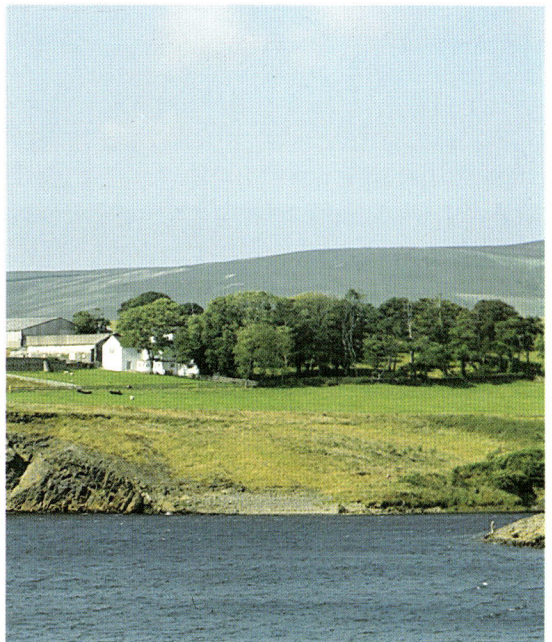

The beautiful view from the rear of the farm

Druidale, on the borders of Lezayre and Michael, is one of the modern names substituted for older Manx ones by new residents of the eighteenth century, and this probably means that the present house, a large one for an old mountain farm, was a replacement during the latter half of the 1700s of an older and smaller one, though no actual building date is available.

The estate itself combines two ancient holdings of mountain land, originally used mainly for summer grazing and for the cutting of turf for winter fuel, and known as Eary or shieling. One was Eary Horkell, a combination of the Gaelic term Eary with the Norse name Thorkell (now Corkill), probably that of the first recorded holder. The other was Eary Kellue, a Gaelic surname now extinct in the Island. Which of the two names was used for the original house on the site of the present one is uncertain, but it is likely to have been Eary Horkell, being on that part of the land.

Ellerslie Manor, Marown

Ellerslie Manor was known for centuries as Ballakilley, meaning Church Farm, and from early times it has been closely connected with the Manx Church. Along with the adjacent estate of Cooilingil, it was granted to the Lord Bishop of Sodor and Man in the eleventh century as part of his Barony lands, and in 1231 Pope Gregory IX confirmed the grant, naming both estates.

Ballakilley was one of the places at which the half-yearly Bishop's Barony Courts were held which dealt with all matters relating to the Bishop's lands. Any changes of tenants had to be approved by the Court and recorded, and rents and 'customs' (payment in kind) were collected at these Courts. The first tenant of Ballakilley on record is one Thomas Moore, but in 1660 the Moores sold out to William Christian of Maughold, a connection of Illiam Dhône, whose widow claimed the estate at a Barony Court in Peel in 1702. The Christian family held the estate until 1823, and later owners have been Anthony Dunlop, William Turnbull and Joseph Faulder, who changed its name to Ellerslie about the middle of the last century, though Manx people still often speak of it as Ballakilley.

In 1898 it was purchased by the late Joseph Cunningham, founder of the Douglas Holiday Camp, and developed as a model farm for the supply of produce to the Camp. Thereafter it returned to the ownership of the original Christian family.

It is still one of the foremost farms in the Island.

Farmhill Manor, Braddan

Farmhill Manor was formerly known as Ballaquirk and was the property of the Quirk family from 1430 to about the middle of the eighteenth century when it passed to Receiver-General Senhouse Wilson. He had settled in the Island through a family connection, Bridget Senhouse, who married John Christian of Milntown in 1717. It was the Wilsons who changed the name to Farmhill, in line with a trend which obtained here in the eighteenth century to supplant as far as possible the original Manx names with English ones. Quite a number of the English gentry had at that time married into Manx families, and it was mainly due to their influence that it became fashionable to imitate English ways and names as a qualification for acceptance in the social life centred on Castletown and its garrison.

Some of the old Manx families held aloof from that circle, and so did the general Manx public. Their allegiance was only to those of the old families who kept to the old way of life, the old estate names and the clan-relationship with their neighbours, often stubbornly refusing to use the new English names for estates such as Ballaquirk, which once played an important part in the Manx ecclesiastical law as the site of a Bishop's Barony Court.

These Courts were first established by Bishop Simon, the man who started building St. German's Cathedral but did not live to finish it. In 1231 he secured from Pope Gregory IX a Bull granting to him and his successors for ever a yearly revenue from certain Church properties in the Island which have ever since been known as the Bishop's Barony. Besides securing the revenue, he established the Barony Courts and created laws and regulations which ensured that the revenue would be duly and regularly collected. The tenants of these Bishop's Barony lands held their estates under the Bishop and not from the Lord of Mann, so these lands were not affected by the Act of Settlement made in 1704 when tenants of the Lord agreed to give him double rent.

Two Barony Courts were held in each year, in May and October, some at Bishopscourt, others at Peel, Braddan, The Nunnery, Kirk Arbory and Castle Rushen. The Braddan ones were held at Ballaquirk, and at least a hundred people would attend a normal court, so it was a memorable occasion for the Bishop's tenants. It was a rule that a Court Dinner be prepared for those coming from a distance, and their ponies were stabled and fed while the Court was in session. These Courts continued to be held up to the mid-nineteenth century, and only Manx Gaelic was used for conducting their business, though the records were kept in Latin. Besides their official business, they provided a big *Giense* for singing, dancing and story-telling before the company dispersed. No doubt there were also a few fights, when people were dissatisfied with the Court's ruling on their disputes — but they must have been much more colourful affairs than are Court proceedings today.

A courtyard at the back of the house makes a very pleasant sun-trap

Glen Garwick, Baldrine

Glen Garwick, Baldrine

Glen Garwick is now a private house but to countless visitors in the past it was known as the Garwick Glen Hotel, although the accommodation for staying guests was extremely limited.

The house lies in a secluded glen with the River Gawne winding through a natural setting of landscaped grounds and passing through a pool before dropping down the delightfully wooded glen to the sea. Pleasant though it undoubtedly is, with its romantic wishing stone, and the Chibbyr Crauee or Well of Wisdom for solving problems, its reputation as a centre for smuggling operations in the eighteenth century is impressive, though it may be largely grounded in imagination rather than history. A cave on the beach is known locally as Dirk Hatterick's Cave and is said to have been the haunt of this notorious smuggler who, apart from being a free trader between the Manx and Galloway coasts, was suspected of being a pirate too. Described by Sir Walter Scott as 'half Manx, half Dutch, half Devil', it is said that in the Island he was regarded as a hero, but in

Glen Garwick as an hotel in the heyday of tourism

Galloway the mere mention of his name was enough to frighten small children. The passageway from the cave up into the glen has long since been blocked up, but the inland end has an imposing entrance some ten feet high.

There are still the remains of an ancient Celtic fortress where a chieftain and his family lived in comparative comfort and safety; and there is the cave in which, according to legend, a hermit sheltered a lady in distress — the Duchess of Gloucester — who had escaped from the dungeons of Peel Castle. She is said to have been hidden there for a year before being recaptured whilst trying to get to England. She spent the rest of her life in the Peel Castle dungeons.

The property's title deeds date back to 1885 but as the old coaching road ran past its front door, it did not remain as a private residence. It soon became a coaching house and then with various changes of ownership, eventually evolved into a small hotel restaurant.

In its heyday as a tourist attraction, visitors would alight from the Manx Electric Railway, pay their entrance money, and spend their time enjoying all the amenities of the glen; playing tennis, having tea by the river or enjoying the rowing boats on the lake or from the beach. There was also the maze modelled on the Hampton Court one in which young couples could hide themselves from their parents.

Garwick is a half Celtic, half Norse word; the first syllable derives from the Gaelic 'coar' — meaning 'pleasant' — and the second from the Scandinavian 'vik' which means 'bay'.

A swimming pool has been added as a north wing to the house

The Wishing Stone on which has been carved the following delightful verses:

Let not Ambition shape your wish,
*   Or you will surely rue it,*
Nor Avarice prompt some wild desire,
*   For you will not come to it —*
The Fairies aid no sordid thought,
*   But firmly would subdue it.*

Brave youth, if maiden's heart you seek,
*   And would aspire to win it,*
Then tarry not to lay your seige,
*   But eagerly begin it:*
The wish that springs from honest love
*   Is granted in a minute!*

Fair maid, your case is in our care,
*   Your wish is ever tender _*
No selfish maiden ever yet
*   Found fairy to befriend her;*
Wish on, and give his name to us —
*   We'll teach him to surrender.*

And ye of middle age who seek
*   The fairies' intercession,*
Let no vain thought of idle wealth
*   Have place in your confessions —*
For happiness and length of years
*   Are far more fair possessions.*

Glentrammon Mansion House or Glentrammon West

Glentrammon Mansion House, Lezayre

Glentrammon Mansion House was originally one quarterland, held in 1511 by Ffinlo Quayle, but it now comprises three houses, each of which has a portion of land. The oldest of these, now called Glentrammon West, was occupied by the Quayle family until the second half of the nineteenth century, and one of them operated a tanyard and bark mill in the glen behind the house until 1851, or possibly a little later. The dwelling house was considerably enlarged sometime within the next decade and the tannery ceased to operate.

In 1851 the main estate was owned by John Corlett, and a new house was built which is probably the one known as Glentrammon Abbey or Glentrammon East. Later, this house also was improved and added to by Parker Mylchreest, a son of the well known 'Diamond King' who lived there for some time.

The third Glentrammon, on the north side of the main road, also an old building but of uncertain date, was owned at the beginning of the last century by James Clarke. There is also Glentrammon Ard, now called Upper Glentrammon, on the uplands at the top of the glen, but no dwellinghouse now remains on this. The quarterland is a very old holding, given in the Chronicle of Man in 1376 as Glen na Droman.

Government House, Onchan

Government House, the official residence of the Lieutenant Governor of the Island, was formerly — in fact still is — Bemahague, one of the old principal estates of the Island dating from Norse times. The name is a combination of Gaelic and Norse elements, which probably means that it was in use in a slightly different form long before the Norse settlements of the ninth century. The first syllable is the Scandinavian prefix 'By' found in a number of Manx place names and meaning a large farm or estate; the rest of the name is Gaelic, from Mac Thaidhg, son of Taig, and the original form was probably Balla(T)haig. The personal name Taig has now become Keig in the Island, and this family were apparently the first holders of the property; but since 1511, the earliest Manorial Roll, it had been held by the Christians. In 1789 however Edward Christian was forced to sell it to Robert Heywood, a wealthy Douglas merchant, for £1,000 to redeem a mortgage.

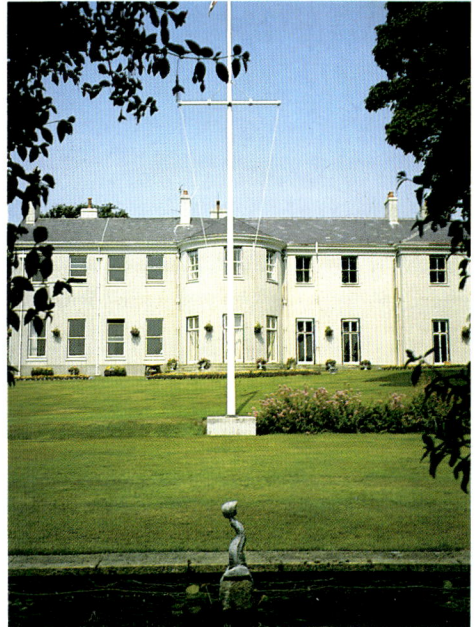

The east face of the house

Robert Heywood rebuilt the original dwellinghouse, and no trace of it can now be identified, though at least part of it must have been incorporated into the present house, and it is believed that some of the outbuildings are those belonging to the original one.

On Robert Heywood's death, Bemahague passed to his son, Deemster John Joseph Heywood, who in turn left it to his married daughter, Mrs. Daly. She left it to her son Francis, who was a minor when he inherited, and before he reached his majority his Trustees leased it in 1863 to Governor Loch, the first Governor to reside at Douglas instead of Castletown. In 1871 Tynwald passed an Act confirming the lease to the Treasurer of the Isle of Man for 21 years at an annual rental of £200, the lessee to contribute £1,000 to the cost of such alterations and repairs as were considered necessary to make it a suitable residence for the Governor. A further lease of 21 years was signed on behalf of Tynwald in 1890, and a further £1,000 was voted for alterations. The lease was transferred to the then newly appointed Government Property Trustees in 1891, but it was not until 1903 that Mr. Daly parted with the house and 112 acres of adjoining land for the sum of £12,000. Between 1903 and 1906 further alterations and extensions were carried out, and the gardens were greatly improved and extended by Governor Lord Raglan.

The entrance hall

Photo: Manx Experience

Until 1919 the Governor had to provide his own furnishings and staff, but today he is entitled under the terms of his appointment to a fully furnished house, though he still has to pay the house staff. The outside staff is paid by the Government.

Several Governors' Ladies have left their mark inside the house. Lady Hill did a great deal to beautify the rooms and installed the beautiful crystal chandeliers from Paris which are in the reception rooms. Lady Granville during her term as chatelaine of Government House embroidered a bedspread and satin hangings for the Tynwald Room for the visit of her sister, now the Queen Mother, in 1945, and Lady Garvey also contributed some beautiful embroideries to the soft furnishings.

For the most recent general redecoration, schemes for both the exterior and interior were designed by the late Mr. John Nicholson, RI, a Fellow of the Institute of British Decorators and Interior Designers, and were carried out by his family firm, Nicholson Brothers.

One of the best known personalities to live in Bemahague before it became Government House was Nessy Heywood, whose heroic efforts to clear the good name of her brother Peter when he was accused of connivance in the mutiny of the *Bounty* — efforts finally crowned with success — have made her a heroine of modern Manx history.

A view from the main reception room, through the drawing room to the dining room beyond.

Photo: Manx Experience

Photo: Henrik Buchleitner

Great Meadow, Malew

Great Meadow is one of the most important estates in the Island and has been continuously occupied since the twelfth century. In 1153 it was listed in a Papal Bull of Eugenius among lands granted by King Olaf of Mann and the Isles to the Abbot of St. Mary of Furness in relation to the Manx Abbey of St. Mary of Rushen adjacent to the estate, which was a daughter house of Furness Abbey. In the *Chronicon Manniae*, the earliest extant history of the Island written by the monks of Rushen Abbey, it is mentioned several times, mainly as a focal point for definition of the Abbey Lands, but as at that time it was the property of the Abbey, no occupant is mentioned. In 1540 when the Abbey was dissolved it was claimed by King Henry VIII of England, but the claim was contested and won by the Manx claimant who stated that he held it under King James of Scotland, and that the English Act in relation to Abbey property had no jurisdiction in the Kingdom of Mann.

In the sixteenth and seventeenth centuries the estate changed hands several times, and in 1703 Francis Wilder Moore of Gillingstone, County Meath, Ireland, is recorded as the owner. He sold it to George Quayle of Castletown, and in 1758 George Quayle undertook by legal agreement to construct a road through his land with 'a proper opening unto the highway, and to build sufficient stone pillars and provide a proper gate eight foot in the clear and sufficiently raised and gravelled.'

At the end of the century the estate came into the possession of the Moores of Billown through a marriage, and in 1790 Thomas Moore of Billown married Emma Hamilton of Scarlett and went to live in Great Meadow.

Their eldest grandson, George, who was born at

Great Meadow in 1853, became a Lieutenant-Colonel in the British Army before taking a seat in the House of Keys. During his period in government, in which he was also a JP, he tried — unsuccessfully — to have all Manx public houses closed down! After his death in 1919 at Great Meadow, his widow continued to live there until she herself died nine years later. Her eldest daughter, Mary Douglas Moore, inherited the estate and married a Surgeon Lieutenant-Commander Robert Riggall RN, and the Moore/Riggall descendants have resided there ever since. There can be few, if any, houses in the Island in which the same family has lived for at least 300 years.

The estate which was originally forty acres in extent has been increased in comparatively recent times to 280 acres and has been a horse stud for the last twenty years. During Word War II, it served as an RAF Officers' Mess.

It has an authentic ghost, a Miss Cregeen who was governess to the Moore children many years ago and was jilted by her fiancé. She scratched her initials on the window of the main staircase, where they can still be seen, went into her bedroom — and just disappeared, never to be seen again except as a ghost which haunts the room.

The Stables

Greeba Castle

Greeba Castle & Greeba Towers, German

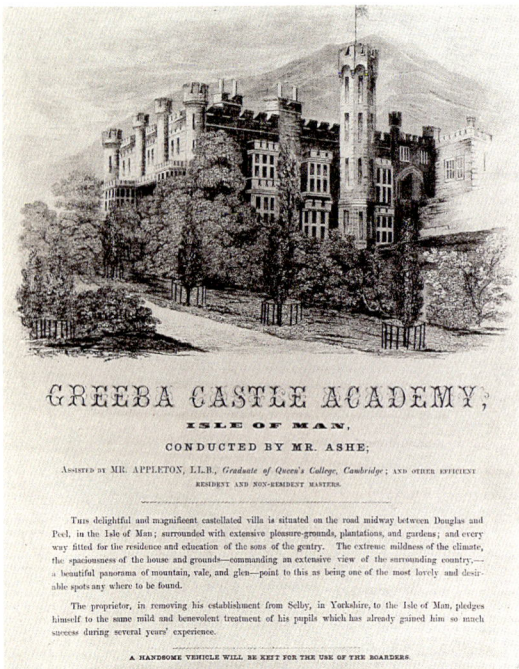

GREEBA CASTLE ACADEMY,

ISLE OF MAN,

CONDUCTED BY MR. ASHE;

Assisted by MR. APPLETON, LL.B., *Graduate of Queen's College, Cambridge*; and other efficient resident and non-resident masters.

This delightful and magnificent castellated villa is situated on the road midway between Douglas and Peel, in the Isle of Man; surrounded with extensive pleasure-grounds, plantations, and gardens; and every way fitted for the residence and education of the sons of the gentry. The extreme mildness of the climate, the spaciousness of the house and grounds—commanding an extensive view of the surrounding country,—a beautiful panorama of mountain, vale, and glen—point to this as being one of the most lovely and desirable spots any where to be found.

The proprietor, in removing his establishment from Selby, in Yorkshire, to the Isle of Man, pledges himself to the same mild and benevolent treatment of his pupils which has already gained him so much success during several years' experience.

A HANDSOME VEHICLE WILL BE KEPT FOR THE USE OF THE BOARDERS.

Photo: Manx Museum & National Trust

The Castle is best known as the residence for some thirty-eight years of the well known Manx novelist, Sir Hall Caine, but perhaps few of the visitors to whom it is pointed out by coach drivers realise that it is practically a twin; that there are in fact two very similar dwellings which may be easily taken for one another on the hillside above the main road from Douglas to Peel. The second house is known as Greeba Towers.

The popular story told by coach drivers as to the reason for this duplication goes as follows:

In the early years of the nineteenth century, England was expecting Napoleonic invasion and some of the wealthy people of the north were acquiring 'bolt-holes' in case it really happened. An English gentleman by the name of William Nowell acquired a property called Booilrenny on the lower slopes of Greeba Mountain for this purpose and built on it a Gothic style residence which eventually came to be known as Greeba Castle in about 1849. But he never lived in it, for the invasion scare abated and, after Waterloo, it was no longer a real threat. One night, Nowell, possibly regretting his investment, sold the Castle for a song whilst in his cups at a party. Later, he tried to retract, but without success. So, as he still held all the surrounding land, he avenged himself on the new owner by building a second almost identical residence cheek-by-jowl with the first one. As Waterloo was won in 1815, the story sounds implausible. Equally, so does another which tells of William Nowell losing the Castle to settle a gambling debt.

Unfortunately, the least romantic story is the most likely. This indicates that after living in Greeba Castle for five years, Nowell and his wife sold it on 1st May 1854 to a Major Thornbury of Spring Valley for £825 — by no means a paltry sum in those days — and Thornbury resold four months later for a £25 profit. William Nowell had however built Greeba Towers before selling the

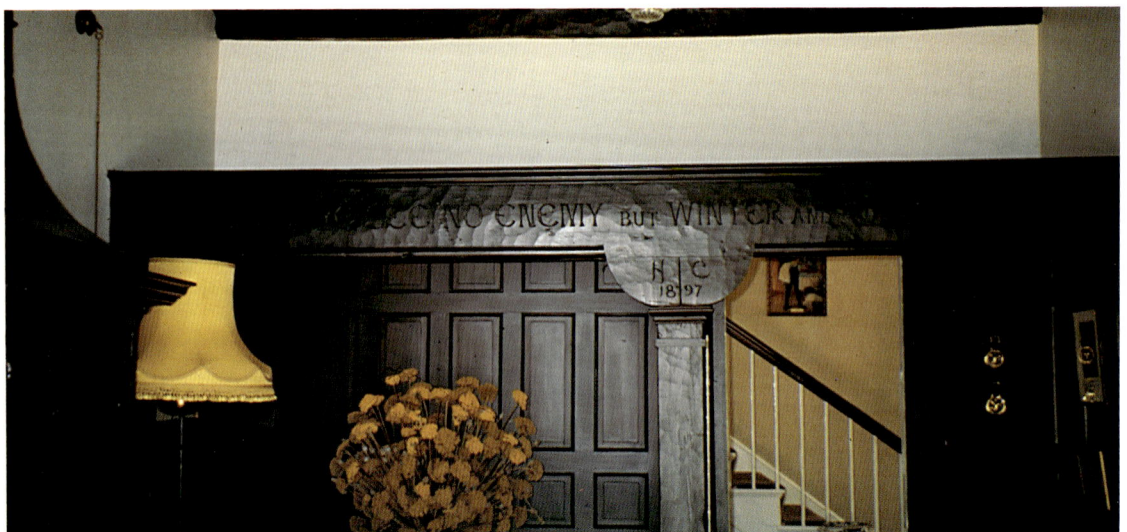

Lintel carving by Hall Caine in the Castle's hall, carved in 1897. 'Here shall ye see no enemy but winter and weather' by William Shakespeare

Greeba Towers

Castle, and he and his wife moved into it upon relinquishing the latter. But Nowell was only able to enjoy it for six years as he died in 1860 aged 40. His widow then let it for many years during which time it became a pleasure resort run by John Clague who also had the pleasure gardens of Glen Helen. But the former venture had a short lived success and Greeba Towers reverted to a boarding house.

In the meanwhile, the purchaser of the Castle, Arbuthnot Emerson of Derby Castle, lived there with his wife until his death. His widow then moved out but retained ownership while it was run as a residential hotel for a number of years. Her children however fell deeply into debt and, in 1879, it was sold by the Coroner under a court order for £800. It continued as a residential hotel until it was bought by a Mr. Ashe who ran it as a boarding school for boys. When that failed, the Castle remained empty for a while. Then in 1887, it was purchased by a Mr. E. W. Windus of the publishing company Chatto & Windus.

In 1895, when Hall Caine was rising rapidly to the summit of his success as a novelist, it was again to let and was rented by him as it was a suitably romantic looking place which would accord well with his public image. A year later he bought it and made it his headquarters for the rest of his life, dying there in 1931.

The Towers had a more conventional history, being sold by private treaty right down to the present time.

Greeba Towers and Greeba Castle c.1880

Hampton Court, Braddan

Hampton Court, near Port Soderick in the Parish of Braddan, was built in about 1800 by Thomas Stowell, one of the foremost Manx Advocates, who was sworn in as Acting Attorney General in 1796 and became Clerk of the Rolls in 1804. He died at Hampton Court in 1821 at the age of 56.

Thomas Stowell's mother, who was Ann Brown before her marriage, was an aunt to the Reverend Robert Brown, the father of T. E. Brown, the Manx poet. The whole family were native speakers of Manx Gaelic, using it habitually in preference to English, and the Reverend Robert Brown, noted for the excellence of his sermons in both languages, was stated by his famous son to have always 'taken more trouble with his Manx sermons than with his English ones', possibly because the majority of his hearers at that time were not so familiar with English as with the old tongue.

Thomas Stowell himself was considered a very able lawyer, and in his office was trained by that famous authority on Manx Law, Sir James Gell. In 1792 Stowell had already published the first alphabetically arranged list of *'The Statutes and Ordinances of the Isle of Man'*, and probably it was his interest in the subject which encouraged Sir James to specialise in it.

But Thomas Stowell did not always live in Hampton Court. His wife died there in 1808 and after that he seems to have resided in Castletown for some years. In the *Manks Advertiser* for 6th February 1813, the estate is advertised to be let and the description reads: 'The Dwelling House contains two kitchens, two parlours, and four bedrooms besides rooms for servants, Store rooms, pantries, cellars, etc. The Offices consist of Coach-house, Stable, Cowhouse and Pidgeonhouse with every convenience for pigs and poultry. The lands consist of thirty-two acres including a Walled Garden and Orchard of about an Acre and a half, all in very good condition:— applications to the Proprietor in Castletown'. It was occupied for some years by one John Abbot, but Stowell was again in residence when he died in 1821, according to his obituary notice in the *Manx Sun.* In 1827 it was advertised for sale as 'That significantly well situated estate, one of the most desirable for its extent in the whole Island comprising a well built handsome Residence suitable for a genteel Family, having most extensive Sea and Land Views, with a large walled Garden and about twenty-six acres of land, well watered and fenced, with a right of Stone Quarry immediately adjoining, and extensive and thriving Plantations.'

Hampton Court was unoccupied for some years and fell into a very dilapidated state. But it has now been renovated to a condition in which it is again a gracious and comfortable family dwelling, not far from Douglas, yet in unspoiled country.

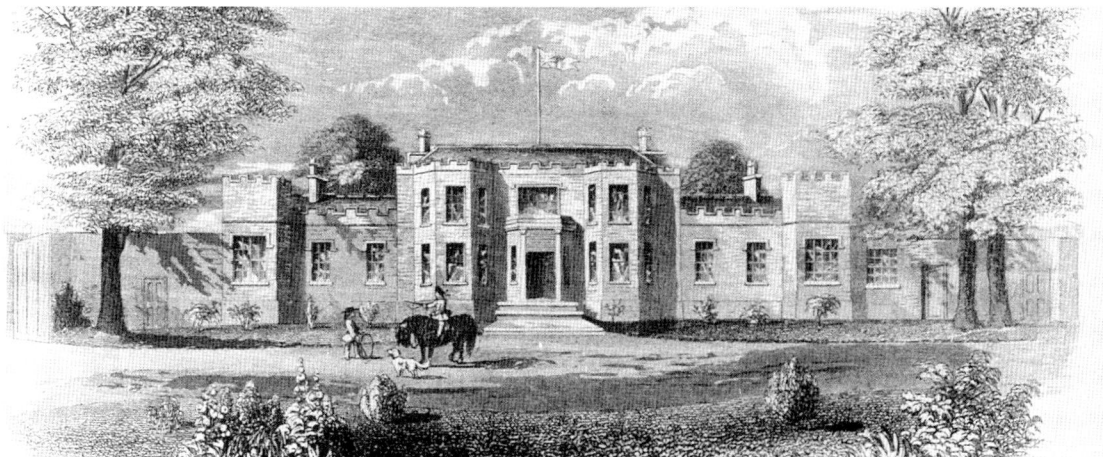

Photo: Manx Museum & National Trust

Harold Tower, Douglas

Harold Tower was built in 1833 for James Newton of Cheadle Heath, Cheshire, who had made money from Liverpool shipping interests and planned to retire to the Isle of Man and live in semi-baronial style; an idea carried out in the style of the building. Apparently, however, monetary reverses resulted in his selling Harold Tower only two years later, and it was bought in January 1838 by High Bailiff James Quirk who went into residence there on 12th May of the same year.

But the most famous person to live in Harold Tower was the well-known English painter, John Martin, who throughout his artistic career concentrated on pictures illustrating Bible themes. In order to find a landscape he considered suitable for each of his major works, Martin used to travel extensively, and the Isle of Man was included in his itinerary. Here, as is well known, he found the landscape which forms the background of one of his most famous paintings, 'The Plains of Heaven'. It was the prospect of the central valley and the mountains to the north of it as seen from the Braaid, Marown. While painting it he lived at Harold Tower.

The dining room

The drawing room

In his heyday, Martin was internationally famous and very highly rated by the art critics. His pictures were exhibited all over the civilised world, and Lord Lytton wrote of 'The Plains of Heaven' that 'it seems the divine intoxication of a soul wrapped in majestic and unearthly dreams, and contains more beauty and tenderness than any other of his works'.

Martin died at Harold Tower on 17th February 1854 after being stricken with paralysis, and was buried at Kirk Braddan. The *Mona's Herald* in an obituary notice praised his work highly and prophesied that his grave would become a place of pilgrimage: but so transitory is artistic fame that today it is difficult to find his headstone, and English critics generally ignore his work.

Yet here the friendly Manx folk are still proud that he chose a Manx scene for a famous work which was shown in many countries. We keep his memory green, and the scene that he painted as his idea of the landscape of Heaven has become one of the showpieces of the coach drivers who point it out regularly to tourists when they take parties over the Braaid road to Foxdale.

Heathfield House, Peel

Heathfield House was built in about 1827 and was owned in 1855 by Henry Corlett Gill, who sold it in that year to William Llewellyn, High Bailiff of Peel for £2,000. It remained in his possession until 1913, when, after Llewellyn's death, it was sold by his family to Mrs. Louisa Campbell Bush for £900, together with eleven acres three roods and seven perches of land which formed the extensive grounds.

High Bailiff Llewellyn actually lived in Castletown, so he rented Heathfield House to a succession of tenants. For many years it was leased as the Peel Vicarage, and five successive vicars of St. German's lived there. It was also rented by Joseph Mylechreest, the 'Diamond King', and he lived there with his family while his new residence, the White House at Kirk Michael was being built.

Mrs. Bush died in 1932 and the house was again offered for sale. It was purchased by Mr. H. S. Cowell, who erected a number of garages on part of the land and ran a haulage business. Mr. and Mrs. Cowell lived in Heathfield House until 1966 when Mr. Cowell retired and sold it.

During the last war Heathfield House was Peel's main centre for charitable efforts of various kinds: garden parties and concerts both indoor and open air.

Injebreck Mansion House, Braddan

Injebreck Mansion House was built in 1810 by James Wade of Port-e-Chee, and in 1813 he planted 200,000 trees on the estate. Probably Wade invested too heavily in these trees, for in November 1814 he advertised the estate and mansion house for sale, but no immediate purchaser was found, and the advertisement was continued for several years. In June 1820 there was a Coroner's sale of stock at Injebreck, and the estate was advertised for letting. In October 1824 it was sold to Mr. Wheatley of Liverpool for £2,100, but apparently he only retained it for something under three years, for by the end of 1827 it was owned by John Abbott. In 1833 the estate was purchased by Alexander Spittall, who was a prominent figure in the Island at that time. The family came originally from Whitehaven, and were Douglas merchants in 1821. They have owned Injebreck since 1833, but Wade's house has been restored and altered several times since it was built.

In the mid-nineteenth century, part of the grounds were leased to a development company which operated it as a pleasure resort that became in the 1880s one of the most popular in the Island. Visitors used to drive out from Douglas by landau or horse-drawn char-a-banc, lunch at the fully licensed residential hotel and drive on to the north of the Island. There was a pavilion for dancing, a seasonal orchestra, pleasure grounds with fountains and rustic pathways, and facilities for games and shooting, with fishing in the Baldwin River. The resident manager was a Robert Mylrea.

Information as to why this attractive resort folded up does not seem to be available; but in 1897 the scheme for the Baldwin reservoir was adopted by the Douglas Corporation, and this may well have been a contributory cause. Today for most people 'Injebreck' connotes the reservoir, inaugurated on 6th September 1905, rather than a residence; but in fact the mansion house is still one of the most attractive and secluded in the Island.

Kirby, Braddan

Kirby has been an important estate from the twelfth century onward. The name comes from the old Norse Kirkju-byr, meaning Church Farm, and it is mentioned in a Papal Bull dated 1231 as Terras de Sti Bradani et de Kyrkbye. In 1405 the mansion house was referred to in an ecclesiastical record as Villa de Kerby, and its owner was bound to entertain the Lord Bishop whenever he left or returned to the Island, sailing from Douglas. This could mean much more than an overnight stay to catch the morning boat, as the sailings were often delayed through bad weather or other causes, sometimes for as long as a fortnight. The entertainment regulation was commuted towards the end of the nineteenth century, a small annual fee being paid to the Church instead.

The present house was built by Colonel Wilks who was to be Governor of the island of St. Helena during the first two years of the exile of Napoleon there in 1815. A desk and the remains of a cellar of real Napoleon Brandy were two mementoes given to Wilks by Napoleon. Following the death of Wilks in 1831 the house was passed to his daughter, Laura, who was then married to General Sir John Buchan. Lady Buchan founded the school at Castletown.

Photo: Manx Museum & National Trust

Colonel Wilks

In 1835 the Buchans leased the house to Sir George Drinkwater who ultimately bought the whole estate in 1840.

Photo: Manx Museum & National Trust

An old print of Kirby seen from the Quarter Bridge

Lewaigue House, Maughold

Lewaigue House has been the seat of a branch of the powerful Christian family from the sixteenth century onward. Ewan Christian of Lewaigue, who lived from 1644 to 1712, was a Member of the House of Keys and Captain of the Parish in 1673. In 1703 he was appointed, along with his relative Ewan Christian of Milntown and John Stevenson of Balladoole, to settle with the Earl of Derby the famous dispute on land tenure in the Island, the settlement they obtained becoming known as the Manx Magna Carta. In 1707 he was one of the appointed delegates from the Keys who asserted the right of the Island to free trading with the UK in a dispute with the British Government, and carried their point.

A descendant of his, another Ewan Christian of Lewaigue (1803-1874) after some years as a soldier of fortune settled at Lewaigue and became a famous Methodist evangelist who had the reputation of being constantly in touch with the spirit world. There are many stories of his dealings, usually effective, with troubled ghosts and even with non-human spirits. He painted right across the front of Lewaigue House the legend: 'Prepare to meet thy God', and it was a well-known landmark for years, but has long since been painted out.

The house was extensively renovated and modernised in the 1970s.

Photo: Manx Museum & National Trust

The house before modernisation

Photo: Manx Museum & National Trust

Lorne House, Castletown

Lorne House is sited on Abbey Land, and was in early times connected with Rushen Abbey. There is a strong tradition of a keeill chapel of the early Celtic church on this site, on the border of the old road separating the Lord's Lands from the Abbey Lands, and this keeill, of which little trace now remains, is still known as Keeill Woirrey, Mary's Church, by old Castletown residents. Lintel graves have been found in the grounds of the existing house, and as late as 1954 drainage excavations in the roadway just outside the grounds exposed a grave of the lintel type.

The existing house was erected in the late eighteenth century and extended in 1828 by a Mr. Cunninghame who lived there for some years, but in 1834 it was acquired as a residence for the Lieutenant Governor, Colonel John Ready, and continued to be Government House until the seat of Government was removed to Douglas.

It is now partly apartments and partly offices.

Milntown, Lezayre

Milntown is one of the most historic houses in the Island. It has been connected for centuries past with the Christian family whose name is closely interwoven with Manx history from Scandinavian times onward. In 1408, when it was owned by Deemster John Christian, it was called Altadale, but in 1530 another Deemster John Christian, his grandson, enlarged the house and planted extensive gardens and parkland, and also improved existing machinery in the old mill, part of the property which had probably operated in a more primitive form long before the Scandinavian settlements.

It was at Milntown, too, that Illiam Dhône Christian, leader of the Manx Rebellion and one of the most dramatic figures in Manx history, spent his boyhood days, and it was in the library there that he was tried for treason against the Lord of Mann in 1662. He met his death in January 1663 by shooting.

In the fifteenth, sixteenth and seventeenth centuries Milntown was used regularly as the meeting place of the Sheading Courts; and in 1776 the John Christian who was then head of the family erected a new battlemented facade. The magnificent bog oak woodwork in the library of the house is said to have come from Close Lake, formerly a part of the Christian lands. And the mahogany doors in the living room came from a wrecked Spanish ship — some say from a vessel of the Spanish Armada wrecked on the Manx

The Mill pond

coast. There is a very strong and persistent tradition all over the Island that such a wreck did actually occur, and that some of the crew and some articles of their property reached the Island, the men settling here and becoming assimilated into the Manx population.

The Christians are no longer in Milntown, though they remained in possession until the early years of the present century, when a lady of the house ran a girls' school there. The last male of the line died at Milntown in 1918 and since then it has been an hotel for a time, but has now reverted to

The Mill lead

The Mill

private ownership. The house and gardens have been restored to their former beauty and order, many young trees having been planted to succeed, in due course, the existing fine old ones which are probably some of those planted in 1530 by Deemster John Christian.

The Nunnery, Braddan

The Nunnery, just outside Douglas, is one of the three oldest ecclesiastical foundations to be continuously occupied from the twelfth century onward, the other two being Rushen Abbey and Bishopscourt; but the present mansion house only dates from the early years of the last century, and only the ancient St. Bridget's holy well and parts of the restored chapel survive of the original convent founded between 1187 and 1190 by Aufrica, sister of King Reginald of Mann and the Isles and wife of John de Courcy of Ulster in fulfilment of a vow.

The estate was held by the Taubmans from 1797, and in 1829 Lieutenant General Goldie, whose family had inter-married with the Taubmans, gave permission for the two names to be combined. In 1829 the new designation appears for the first time in official records when Captain John Goldie-Taubman was elected a Member of the House of Keys.

The present house is one of the most imposing on the Island, built in baronial style and surrounded by extensive gardens and parklands. It remains a private residence.

The Nunnery from an old print

Oak Hill, Braddan

Oak Hill was formerly Cronk Bane, and under this name it appears in the Manorial Roll for 1643, held by Juan Quilliam. It was known as Cronk Bane, or sometimes Knock Bane, a variant of the name, until 1798 when it came into the possession of a Captain Edward Forbes, who changed its name to Oak Hill.

In 1812 it was owned by John Bell, who also owned several herring houses on the North Quay, Douglas and a fishing boat named the *Loyal Bell*, which was wrecked off Derbyhaven in October 1824. Bell died in September 1829, and Oak Hill was taken by the Reverend B. Philpots in December of the same year. In 1830 he advertised in the *Manx Sun* for a schoolmistress to take charge of a Day and Sunday school in Oak Hill Lodge, which seems to have been one of a number of private schools operating in and around Douglas in the early nineteenth century.

In 1832 part of the farmland was advertised to be let on lease, and in 1833 the house and grounds were let furnished to Sir John Taubman. Later it became a school again, for in 1836 Mr. J. H.

Garvin advertised in the *Manx Sun* that he had 'removed his school from Athol Street to Oak Hill.' Thereafter the building appears to have suffered a disastrous fire and had to be rebuilt. The oldest ruined outbuilding which has recently been restored had the appearance of being a chapel at one time and it seems probable that there has been habitation on the site from very early times.

Photo: Manx Museum & National Trust

A steel engraving of the original Oak Hill building

The Old Vicarage, Maughold

The Old Vicarage is a gracious dwelling probably built, or rebuilt, to incorporate an earlier house in the early eighteenth century. It has housed many successive vicars of Kirk Maughold, but has recently been superseded in this function by an adjacent modern house, though it is still in private occupation. The Manx poet 'Cushag' (Josephine Kermode) and her famous brother P.M.C. Kermode, lived there in their youth when their father was vicar of Maughold, and many of 'Cushag's' poems have the parish of Maughold as their background.

Ormly Hall, Lezayre

Ormly Hall was formerly Ballaclaghbane, which is Manx Gaelic for Whitestone Farm, and there must have been a farmhouse on the estate before it was bought by Mr. Paton, father of the Reverend George Paton, vicar of St. Paul's, Ramsey, who came to the Island to retire and built the present house about 1850, naming it Ormly Hall. Whether or not any of the former building is incorporated in the present house seems to be unknown. In 1852 George Paton, then a youth of about 18, arrived to spend a vacation with his parents. He had to land from the steamer in a small boat, and to his surprise found the sea front, harbour and quays decorated and flying flags: it was the day on which the pleasure steamer 'Manx Fairy' sailed into Ramsey for the first time.

Mr. Paton senior died in 1860, and in 1902 the house was taken over by the Quayle family, who ran a bakery there for some forty years, but between the death of Mr. Paton and their occupancy, there is a considerable gap about which no information seems to be available.

Some of the furniture from Ormly Hall was acquired by The Manx Museum Trustees for the T. E. Brown Memorial Room, presumably because it had at one time belonged to, or been used by, the Manx poet himself.

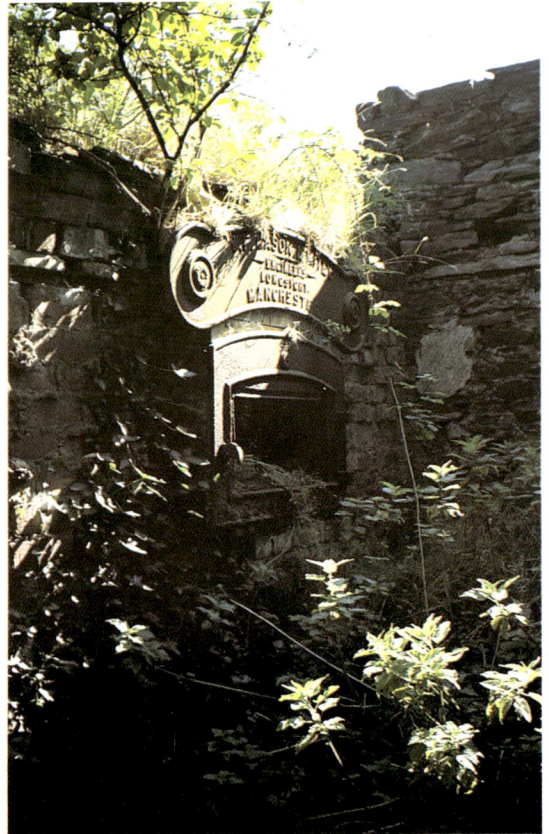

The remains of the Quayle family's baking ovens can still be seen in a secluded part of the garden.

Orrisdale House, Michael

O rrisdale House or Oristal as it appears in the old records until 1775, is probably the modern counter-part of an early Viking settlement and residence, for many Norse artifacts have been unearthed on the estate, and where it touches the coast a number of pre-Christian and early Christian burials have been found.

When Colonel Richard Townley toured the Island in 1789 and later published a Journal of his itinerary, he visited Orrisdale, then owned by Deemster John Frissell Crellin, who took him round the objects of antiquarian interest on the estate, and the one which seems to have impressed Townley most was 'a fine level clod upon the lofty beach which was perfectly level, smooth and circular; elevated to above the surrounding surface of the ground........ surrounded first by a regular excavation (from which it has acquired its elevation) and then by a regular mound entirely corresponding with the inward circle.' There has, however, been much erosion of the coast in this area, and this striking earthwork has entirely disappeared.

The Crellins have held Orrisdale for over two hundred years and are one of the most distinguished families in the north of the Island. Some of the family migrated to Ballachurry, Andreas, but, after extensive renovation, the old Orrisdale house remains in Crellin hands. It is located in one of the most charming and secluded nooks of the west coast, and is typical of an old Manx mansion house belonging to an influential family.

An unusual three-dimensional model of the house as it was originally built

89

Parville, Arbory

Parville seems at first sight a modern name, but in fact it appears in the Liber Episcopii (Book of Bishops) for 1587, when it was held by Deemster John Parr, who used the Latin 'villa' in coining a name for his house which would incorporate his own surname, in place of the usual Manx 'balla', probably through ecclesiastical influence.

Later the property came into the possession of the Cooils, a well-known Arbory family, some members of which were Members of the House of Keys and Captains of the Parish. They retained the original name — which in fact has never been changed right down to the present day — though the house has changed hands several times. In the early years of the last century it was owned by a Dr. Quillan reputed to be a scholarly philologist; after his time it became a boarding house for a while, and in the 1920s it reverted to the Cooil family. The last of them to live there was a Mr. Robert Cooil, senior partner in a big Manchester business firm who used to commute every week-end.

Parville has one of the most colourful gardens in the Island

Port-e-Chee Farmhouse, Braddan

Port-e-Chee, a farmhouse situated on a beautiful and extensive stretch of meadowland known as the Port-e-Chee Claddagh, just outside Douglas, is one of the few large dwellings which have suffered little change in either structure or name for some two hundred years. Only the spelling of the name has been changed — the Manx form is *Purt-y-Shee*, which Victorian sentimentality likes to translate as 'Harbour of Peace' — but which originally meant 'Fortress of the Fairies'. It was chosen by the Duke of Atholl on his accession as Lord of Mann to be his personal dwelling, and he, being a good Gael, kept to the existing Gaelic name of the property instead of, as was then fashionable, renaming it in a rather hit-or-miss translation. He bought it in 1791 from P. Tobin for £3,500, and gave Mrs. Tobin another £100 'with which to purchase a gown, as is the custom in the country from which I come'. With the house the Duke took over 'all the wines, stock and furniture therein'.

But His Grace did not live at Port-e-Chee for very long periods; much of his time was spent in Scotland and England. So he lent it as a residence to his relative, Lord Henry Murray. But when, in 1793, the Duke desired to spend a summer holiday in the Island and gave Lord Henry notice to vacate the house temporarily, his request was refused. Lord Henry then bought the small property named Newton in Santon and moved out for good, taking away all the furniture and effects, probably including some of the furniture taken over at its purchase by the Duke, leaving the house, according to the Duke's agent, 'utterly dismantled', the only provisions left there being four hams, four loaves of sugar, two fat bullocks and ten fat wethers.'

After a time the Duke decided to let Port-e-Chee, and its first tenant, in 1802, was James Bonnyman. In 1810 it was occupied by John Wade, chiefly remembered for his extensive plantings of trees, some around Port-e-Chee and about 200,000 at Injebreck.

The elegant drawing room

From 1722 there had been among the small houses on the Port-e-Chee land a cottage industry in spinning, weaving, printing and making up cotton and linen. In 1816 the Duke's agent, James Macrone, a keen businessman, tried to persuade His Grace to extend this into a large factory, but met with some discouragement. He continued to press his plan, however, and by 1822 had apparently secured enough support to insert a notice in the *Isle of Man Advertiser* that 'The Governor in chief intends to establish a linen manufactory on an extensive scale on Port-e-Chee Claddagh.' What happened after that does not seem to have been recorded, but the plan was never carried out, probably owing to a veto by the Duke, who disliked the idea of a factory on that site.

In 1834 the Duke sold Port-e-Chee to Sir George Drinkwater of Kirby, and since then it has passed through a number of hands.

The snug television room with a beautiful stone chiollagh stretching across the width of the room

Pulrose Manor House, Braddan

Pulrose Manor House was originally called by the Manx Gaelic name Pooyll Roach, and in almost this form it appears in the Manorial Roll of 1643 — Poleroach, meaning Pool in the Wood, which is quite an apt description of what must have been a prominent feature of the estate at that time. A later spelling was Pulrosh, and it was only in the first decade of the last century that the present form was adopted. It has nothing to do with the botanical species rose.

The principal family associated with Pulrose is that of the Moores, who also held Cronkbourne. Nobody really knows where they originated, but it was probably in Ireland, where the Moores were a powerful clan. Anyway, from medieval times they appear prominently in the annals of Liverpool, and in the early sixteenth century they settled in the Island and soon began to take an equally prominent part in Manx affairs. In 1525 William Moore, MHK purchased Pulrose from Robert Standish, a member of the same family as Myles Standish, the Pilgrim Father, American colonist and military leader of the Plymouth colony in New England. From then until the early years of the present century it was held by the Moore family. One of them, John Moore of Pulrose married a daughter of the famous Manx naturalist, Professor Edward Forbes, and the last of the Moores, Marion Margaret, born in 1847 and married to Bell Graham Williams in 1869, died there on 6th May 1905.

After passing through various hands, the estate was acquired by the Douglas Corporation in 1927 and the surrounding land developed as a housing estate, the first one built as an extension of Douglas. Almost hidden by the new development, the old house, however still stands among old trees, a relic of the days when Douglas was surrounded by large, comfortable Victorian estates with their gardens and parklands interspersed with flourishing farms.

The pool which gives the estate its name seems to be a large one in the River Glass, and in 1824 a man was drowned trying to ford it on horseback during a river flood. His horse swam to safety in one of the Pulrose fields.

Photo: Manx Museum & National Trust

A photograph of the Manor House taken around 1950

The Raggatt, Peel

The Raggatt has been the residence of several important local families. The name is derived from the Scandinavian Rärgata, which means Roe-track, and it is situated close to an old road leading to a pool in the River Neb where tradition says the deer from King's Forest on the adjacent hillsides used to come down to drink in the days of the Kingdom of Mann and the Isles.

In the early nineteenth century the house was owned by William Bridson MHK whose daughter married one Captain Ewen Cameron of Glen Nevis. Captain Cameron later inherited The Raggatt through his wife and came to live there, eventually becoming Captain of the Parish of Patrick, holding that office until his death. By 1871, however, he had moved to Glenfaba House and had apparently let The Raggatt to a Mr. Southey. Later residents were named Kaye and Watterson, and one Isabel Kelly is recorded as part owner in 1889.

It is said that when Cromwell's forces were shelling Peel Castle into submission in 1651 they stabled their horses at the house.

Ravenscliff, Douglas

Ravenscliff is said to be one of 'the five original mansions of Douglas', but there seems to be no record of the date when it was built. The existing house seems characteristic of the early 19th century, and it is admirably situated with an unrestricted view over the harbour and bay, yet surrounded on three sides by trees where the ravens which gave the house its name are still seen occasionally. Sheltered by the high cliffs of Douglas Head behind, it also has a high stone wall, so the gardens are well protected.

Photo by courtesy of Stowell Kenyon

The Rectory House, Andreas

Rectory House is the present building on the site of a dwelling place which goes a long way back into Manx history. The first Rector of Andreas was named Deremod (Old Gaelic Diarmid, modern Gaelic Kermode), and he was appointed in 1188 A.D. His rectory survived until 1645, when Samuel Rutter, a poet and playwright who later became Bishop, was Archdeacon of Man; and in 1666 it was rebuilt by his successor, William Urquhart. A number of alterations and additions have been made since then but the foundations of an older building have recently been uncovered.

An inventory made in 1677 provides an interesting glimpse of Manx houses of the better sort in the seventeenth century. It mentions that the rectory had five rooms; the *Thie Mooar*, equivalent to the Great Hall; the *Greinnagh*, or Sunny Place, a very old Gaelic name for a room set apart for the ladies of the family and more or less the equivalent of the modern drawing-room; the *Chamyr*, or study; the *Chamyr Seose*, or main bedroom, and the *Chamyr Beg*, or small bedroom. The *Thie Mooar* served as a common room, refectory and kitchen, and held two long trestle tables, a small round table, two cupboards, a linen press, two armchairs, a settle, two chests and several stools, with spinning wheels for flax, hemp and wool. The *Chamyr* had an oak table, a chest, a settle, two armchairs and several stools, and the *Chamyr Seose* and *Chamyr Beg* had wooden bedsteads with feather mattresses, chests and stools.

The *Thie Mooar* was flagged, and the usual practice was to cover the flags each morning with fresh rushes after sweeping out and burning those used the day before. The other rooms had green velvet curtains and carpets. In the *Thie Mooar* there was a big *chiollagh*, or open hearth and chimney, on which the cooking was done, and the social life of the household centred in this room beside the fire of peat and wood. Clocks were scarce, and a sundial was relied upon for a record of the time by the household, while for the information of outside workers bells were rung in the early morning, at noon, and at the hour for ceasing field work. The rectory estate included a small farm with cattle, horses, sheep, poultry and bees to supply the household, and the rector also kept a small fishing-boat at the Lhen Beach.

During the last war the rectory was used as an RAF officers mess, then became a youth hostel from 1945 to 1953.

*A stiffly posed Victorian photograph of a group
at the front door of Rectory House*

Riversdale, Lonan

Riversdale was built about the end of the eighteenth century for the Reverend William Fitzsimmons, a well known character who wrote a history of the Island and was elected to the House of Keys in 1806.

Later, about the middle of the last century, it became a restaurant and place of entertainment for summer visitors. At that time horse-drawn char-a-bancs used to make the trip round Glen Roy from Laxey; the upper part of the glen was laid out with footpaths and seats with a playground for children, and a small charge was made for entering. The trip was reckoned a day's entertainment; the horses were put up and fed in the extensive stables of Riversdale, meals were served in the house with a small concert party to provide entertainment; a couple of hours were left free for ramblage, and then the parties returned to Laxey via Ballacowin and Baldhoon. With the development of the more convenient Laxey Glen Gardens opening in the village, however, the trade of Riversdale declined, and it eventually closed down, the house becoming a private residence again.

Scarlett House, Malew

The Conservatory

S carlett House, near Castletown, has the distinction of having virtually grown out of the rocks on which it stands, for it is built of Scarlett limestone and looks completely native. The quarry from which its materials were taken was in full operation in the late eighteenth century, and it was built about the turn of the century. In 1803 it was advertised to let, and in 1805 John Prockton of Scarlett House offered a remedy for the disease of 'smut' in wheat to the Manx farmers. It then passed into the hands of the Vicar General, the Reverend Ewan Christian, who died there in 1808, after which half the estate and the house were offered for letting and it became a superior boarding house, one resident, probably a retired Army officer, advertising himself as prepared to give French lessons.

In the early years of the present century it was occupied by a lady well known in Manx antiquarian circles, Mrs. Narramore, who was connected with the famous Castletown ship-owning family, the Karrans.

A magnificent view of Castletown Bay can be had from the front of the house

Southampton , Braddan

Southampton, on the old Castletown Road, is part of the Hampton estates which included Hampton Court, Hampton Villa, Hampton Cottage and Southampton. All of these houses appear to have been built and renamed in the first decade of the nineteenth century by one Matthew Hampton, who lived at Southampton until his death at the age of 93 in 1822. The whole property was formerly the farm Ballaquiggin.

In the same year (1822) Southampton was bought by John Atkinson, who seems to have let it, along with Hamppon Court, to a Mr. May who ran a private school in Douglas called the Douglas Academy. May developed on the estate a new branch of his school, which was a large and highly successful one, and named the new section the Hampton Court Academy. Classes were held in Hampton Court itself, and Southampton was used as accommodation for the resident pupils.

The original farm, Ballaquiggin, appears in the Manorial Roll for 1643, when it was held by one John Quiggin for whom it was named; but no trace of the original house now remains.

Matthew Hampton was Coroner of Middle Sheading in 1803, and was a subscriber to *Mills' Statute Laws*. The first Hamptons are recorded in Braddan in the mid-eighteenth century, and they seem to have remained in that parish and married into the Bridson Quayle families.

Thornhill Manor, Lezayre

Thornhill, though not an historic house in the sense in which the adjective may be applied to Milntown or Bishopscourt, has been one of the most important estates in the north of the Island for the past hundred years as the home of a family which has given several successive members to the House of Keys and has borne a prominent part in Manx affairs generally. It is sited on the quarterland of Ballacarbary in the Treen of Grest, and was built by Mr. William Callister MHK on land acquired by him, between August 1844 and July 1845. Mr. Callister and his family took up residence, but only, at first, for the summer months. This is an example of what seems today a somewhat extraordinary custom which obtained during the nineteenth century, and perhaps earlier, among the landed gentry of the north, most of whom used to live in their 'town house' in Ramsey during the winter months and move out to their main country residence about Whitsuntide. Although most of these estates were only a few miles out of the town, road conditions and country conveniences were far from today's standards, and distances took much longer to cover, so perhaps the custom was not so pointless as it now seems.

The original house consisted of a porch, hall with a large dining room opening off it on one side and an equally large drawing room on the other, while also on the ground floor were a smoke room and a spacious kitchen with a butler's pantry and scullery. On the first floor were four main bedrooms, a dressing room, bathroom and separate toilet. The second floor had three staff bedrooms and an attic. There were also three separate cellar rooms, one for wine, one used as a laundry, and the third for storage of wood and seeds. There were many specimen trees in the extensive grounds, collected by members of the family from Africa and many other parts of the world, and beside the ornamental gardens, in which was a 'log-cabin' summerhouse, there was a big walled garden for fruit trees and bushes and vegetables. Some years after its erection a three storey rear wing was added to the house, and there was also stabling at the back.

An indication of the importance with which Thornhill and its occupants were regarded in Victorian times is the fact that one of the few early letter-boxes around Ramsey was set into its gate-post. Mr. William Callister, its builder, was Member of the House of Keys for Ayre, and he was succeeded in the House by his son-in-law, Mr. Thomas Clucas, and later by his grandson, John Donald Clucas.

Upper Kerrowglass, Michael

Upper Kerrowglass was for many years occupied by the Faragher family who were well known as preservers of Manx folklore and songs and were often visited by collectors such as the late Sophia Morrison, William Cubbon of the Manx Museum and Walter Gill, author of the Manx Scrap Books.

Like many of the old Manx farm cottages it was sold and subsequently enlarged and modernised.

The White House, Michael

T he White House was built in the eighteenth century. Notable occupiers were the Taubmans, later of the Nunnery; Sir Mark Wilks, Napoleon's gaoler on St. Helena, who later moved to Kirby; Captain Quilliam of Trafalgar fame, who died there. During the nineteenth century it was farmed by Evan Gell who developed the shorthorn breed of cattle on the Island, and latterly was bought by Joseph Mylchreest, a Peel man, who spent much of his working life in the African diamond business and became a friend of Cecil Rhodes. Mylchreest added a Victorian wing to the property (since demolished), and lived there till his death in 1896. Much of the existing house is the original Georgian with additions from Victorian times to date.

An old print showing the house as it was originally built, with an imposing tower over the front entrance and the upstairs floor continued over to the left of the tower.

Woodlands, Douglas

The drawing room

Woodlands was built by John Archibald Brown, Editor of the *Isle of Man Times*, in 1899 and was the Brown family residence for many years.

The Browns of the Times were one of the best-known families in Manx business, the official name of the firm being The Isle of Man Times Ltd., Brown and Sons, General Printers, publishers and newspaper proprietors. Its founder was James Brown who came to Douglas from Liverpool to work as a jobbing printer in 1846, and in 1848 started a small newspaper called the '*Manx Lion*' in a printing office which he had acquired in Duke's Lane. This little paper, described as 'Liberal', only lasted for a few

The dining room

months, and no copy of it is now known to exist, though there are a number of references to it available. After its demise in 1848, Brown went on the staff of the original *Isle of Man Times*, which was published in 1847 by William Sherrifs and Andrew Russell. This firm shortly became insolvent, and Brown transferred to the *General Advertising Circular*, which he took over in 1855 in settlement of a debt, and continued it under the same title until he merged it into the new *Isle of Man Times*, the first issue of which appeared on 4th May 1861.

The impressive hall and minstrel's gallery

Woodland Towers, Onchan

Woodland Towers, one of the baronial style houses which were popular in the Island in the late eighteenth and early nineteenth centuries, is best known as the residence of one of the most extraordinary Manxmen of modern times. He was William Henry Abdullah Quilliam, born on 10th April 1856 in Onchan. But he claimed he was of Hungarian birth, was related to the Hungarian royal family, and took the name of Quilliam from his mistress in Liverpool where he finished his education and where he was, in 1878, called to the Bar.

Scion of a Methodist family, Quilliam became a Moslem following a visit to Morocco, and went to Persia in 1889 where he was entertained by the Shah. On his return, he was appointed Persian Vice-Consul in Liverpool, and in 1890 he was a guest of the Sultan at the Palace of Yildiz. Later he went to Afghanistan, where he was decorated by the Prince and invested with the Order of Kolah-u-Izzai. He published a number of books dealing with the religions of both eastern and western worlds, became a Sheik, and made a pilgrimage to Mecca.

But as if this were not sufficient in the way of unusual enterprise for one man, in about 1912 he changed his name after marrying a French lady, in order to conform with the conditions of a will — and thenceforward he lived as a double personality; Sheik Abdullah Quilliam, head of the Moslems of Great Britain, and William Henri Marcel Leon, MA, LLD, Medaille des Beaux Arts (Constantinople), Izzai Medal in Gold (Afghanistan) and several other honours, Dean of the London School of Physiology, a prominent freemason, and a member of the Celtic section of the International Society of Philology and Fine Arts — all honours and positions which he had won by his own enterprise.

His first marriage had been to a Miss Kerruish of Ramsey, daughter of a former Speaker of the House of Keys. During the 1914-18 war, he was extremely useful to the Allies in espionage work, receiving a decoration from the king for one particular job in which he had risked his life.

Owing to the change of name and the fact that he had also retained his own name for certain aspects of his work, he was for many years regarded as a mystery man, and it was only when he died in 1932 that the full story was made public. He lived at Woodland Towers from 1903 until his death and established there a Moslem temple or mosque which was attended by members of that faith from Liverpool and the north of England.

He was a prolific writer, and besides his books on religions he wrote several Manx ones: *Manx Antiquities* (1898), *English-Manx-Gaelic Etymologies* (1914) and a *Geology of the Isle of Man* (1915). He was undoubtedly a most brilliant man but he unfortunately became involved in some financial transactions regarded as shady and this probably prevented him from receiving credit for the excellent work he did in other directions.

On his death, his widow sold Woodland Towers to an Arthur Kniveton when it was called 'Onchan

The Cats' Castle. Built by the present owner as a refuge for distressed cats

Towers'. The new owner, an engineer returned from Australia, ran it as an hotel with the emphasis on tennis holidays for which two courts were built. The venture failed because the guests found it too far from Douglas and the sea, and when complaining about the inadequate food as well were told 'But where else can you see such fine pine trees?'

Arthur Kniveton continued to live at the Towers thoughout World War II — during which an unexploded bomb fell from an Allied plane on to the lawn — selling it eventually in 1946 to a retired army Colonel who kept chickens. And during the 1950s it was run as a market garden by a Mr. L. G. Griffiths who built the greenhouses which are still very much in evidence. When that venture too failed, the house was the subject of a forced sale as a result of Griffiths' bankruptcy.

GLOSSARY

GLOSSARY *(Cont.)*